Dying Is Part of This World

KAYLA JARMON

Dying Is Part of This World by Kayla Jarmon
Published by Tamarisk Tree Publishing

www.KaylaJarmon.com

© 2018 Kayla Jarmon

The text of this book is set in 14-point Garamond Light

Book formatting and cover design by jCo Creative
Illustrations © 2018 Piper Mirú

Printed in the U.S.A.

For information about special discounts available
for bulk purchases, sales promotions, fund-raising
and educational needs, contact admin@kaylajarmon.com

First Edition

ISBN: 978-1-948706-01-8

This book exists for God's glory,
and as a tool to carry you to the throne of God
to find mercy and help in the time of need.
Hebrews 4:16

As a child, I feared my mother's death. I would come to her with my fear, and she would tell me not to think about those things… This did little to help me.

When I became a Christian at the age of 27, God's wisdom shed light on many questions that this life holds. As I grew in him, he gave answers to many of my old questions, as well as the new ones that followed. The natural overflow of this wisdom was my living out 2 Corinthians 1:3-4, and this book is part of that process.

Dying is Part of This World sprang from actual conversations with my children. The first one took place in the car, much like this book details with a mother and her child traveling home. It weaves in God's wisdom as they discuss the child's fear of the mother dying.

I've added discussion questions and Scripture references at the end of each chapter. I hope they help you dig deeper in God's Word on this subject.

I pray that in these pages you find comfort surrounding the subject of death, and that it sparks-many conversations that carry you to the throne of God for his wisdom and love.

CONTENTS

Acknowledgments   i

1   Fear of Death   1

2   Remembering   9

3   Preparation Stages   15

4   Time Here and There   23

5   Help When Losing Someone   29

6   The Second Death   35

7   God's Economy   41

ACKNOWLEDGEMENTS

Thanks to all who helped bring this book
to fruition:

To my husband, for giving me support
and space to work out the gifts the Lord
has given me.

To my family, for reading my stories and
encouraging me along the way.

To Ryan and Sarah, your skill sets and
creativity are invaluable to me.

To Piper, for your illustrations. God brought
me a treasure with you.

To Valerie, for your edits and feedback.
I appreciate you so.

To Ann, for allowing me to bounce things
off you and for final edits with this book.

Most of all, thank you Lord for giving us your
wisdom as we seek you.

DYING IS PART OF THIS WORLD

.

CHAPTER ONE
The Fear of Death

"Buckle up, Sweetie."

"I am."

"Did you have fun at Papa's today?"

"Yeah."

"You seem sad. What's wrong?"

"I am sad."

"Why? I thought you had a great day with Papa?"

"I started thinking about you dying."

"What made you start thinking about that?"

"Papa was watching something on the news that made me think about how much I'd miss you, if you died."

"Oh, Sweetie, everyone has to die at some point. That's been part of this world since Adam and Eve sinned."

"I know, but I don't want you to die."

"You know what? We shouldn't waste our time thinking about that. Instead, we should enjoy the time we have together now, in the present."

"I know, but when I see the news it makes me think about it."

"Let me help you then. Think of it like

this: You know where Christians go when they die, right?"

"Yes, they go to be with Jesus in heaven."

"That's right. And all their Christian loved ones will see them again one day, right?"

"Right."

"And when will they see them again?"

"Either when they die or when Jesus comes back, whichever comes first.

Mama, I know all that, but if you died I'd miss you so much. And even if I died first, I'd still miss you from heaven. So no matter what, I'm gonna be sad!"

"Oh, Sweetie, I can see you're upset, but I promise if you went to heaven first, you'd be so happy with Jesus that you wouldn't miss me at all."

"But I know I would."

"I promise you wouldn't. Not only would

you be with Jesus, but you'd be out of this sin-filled world too. In this world many things have gone wrong and go wrong every day. When you see Jesus, all will be made very clear to you, and you won't wonder about anything or miss anyone at all. But if you did think of me while in heaven, you would know that I'd be joining you soon; and "soon" in heaven, where there is no time, is very, very soon indeed."

"What do you mean, 'If I did think of you'? Why wouldn't I think of you? You're my mama. I think about you all the time!"

"And I think of you all the time too, but answer this: How did you become my child?"

"What do you mean?"

"How did you become a member of our family where Daddy and I take care of you?"

"God gave me to you."

"Yes, he did, but how'd you get here?"

"Huh?"

"Did you just appear out of nowhere and all of a sudden you were our child?"

"No, I was born to you."

"What do you mean by 'born'?"

"You know what I mean. I was in your belly and then I was born to you."

"You were actually in my womb, Sweetie, but how do you know you were in my womb? Do you remember being there?"

"No, but I've seen the picture and that video of when I was."

"That's right, the ultrasound picture and video. And who knit you in my womb?"

"God did."

"Yes, and God knew us before our days ever came into being, correct?"

"Yes."

"Well, listen carefully. Everyone who lives

on this earth gets here through the vehicle of a mama and a daddy. The womb is the only natural way for a baby to get here, and it's been that way ever since Adam and Eve. Everyone who lives on this earth was at one time knit together by God, and he uses the mama and daddy to begin that process."

Genesis 3; Corinthians 5:8; 1 Thessalonians 4:15-18; 1 Romans 5:12; 1 Thessalonians 5:9-10; Revelation 22:5; Psalms 139:13, 16-17; Genesis 2:21-24; 3:16

The Fear of Death
Discussion Questions

1. Do you worry about someone you love dying?

2. Where do Christians go when they die?

3. After Christians die, will they see their loved ones again? When?

4. Before any of our days came into existence, who knew us?

5. God knit us together where?

DYING IS PART OF THIS WORLD

CHAPTER TWO
Remembering

"Oh, I remember those days when God was knitting you in my womb. Several of those days, I didn't feel so well. And I would get sad over the smallest, silliest things! And the longer you were in there, the tighter my clothes got; and I had really weird food cravings too, which didn't help.

I remember the first time I felt you kick; everybody put their hands on my belly to feel it too.

Your daddy and I read the Bible to you and prayed over your life every day. We sang to you often, and sometimes when we'd stop singing, you'd start poking me. We knew you wanted us to keep singing because when we'd start back, you'd get still again."

"And I still like to hear you sing, and for you to sing with me."

"I love singing with you too.

Well, the day of your birth drew closer and closer, and we couldn't wait to see you! It finally arrived, and you were born. Everyone was so excited to see you! Those were the good old days. Do you remember any of them?"

"No, but I like it when you talk about them."

"But why don't you remember them? You were there."

"I know I was, but I don't. Do you remember when you were in Mimi's belly? Uh, I mean womb."

"No, I don't but I was there nonetheless, and you were in my womb nonetheless too. I also remember, very clearly, the first three years of your life. Do you remember those years?"

"No, but will you tell me about them?"

"Sure. We took extra special care of you the first year of your life. You seemed so fragile, and with you being our first, everything was so new to us. Every new thing brought us such joy: your first bath, your first smile, the first time you held your head up, the first time you rolled over, the first time you sat up, your first taste of baby food, the first time you said 'ma ma' and 'da da,' the first time you scooted, the first time you stood up by yourself, your first steps, the first time you fed yourself. Those years were packed full of firsts and tons of joy for us! Don't you remember them?"

"I don't, but when we get home, can we watch some of those videos of me doing them?"

"Sure. But why don't you remember those

days, Honey? You were there!"

"I know I was, but I don't remember them. Do you remember any of your first things?"

"No, but I did them nonetheless, and you did too. Whether or not we remember them, we both did them."

"Talking about those days is making me sadder, because I don't want to be away from you."

"Well, Baby, keep listening."

Remembering
Discussion Questions

1. Do you remember kicking your mama when you were in the womb?

2. Do you remember your parents talking to you when you were in the womb?

3. Even if you don't remember being in the womb, what is true?

4. Do you remember your first bath, smile, the first time you sat up or your first steps?

5. Even if you don't remember doing any of your first things in life, you still did them. True or False?

DYING IS PART OF THIS WORLD

CHAPTER THREE
Preparation Stages

"We've talked about how we get here through a mama and a daddy. Before anyone gets here, they must spend time growing in their mama's womb. They grow there every day, and when they're ready for this world, they're born into it. You see, babies are not meant to stay in their mamas' wombs; they're meant to live here in this world.

Could you imagine living in my womb forever?"

"No. And I wouldn't want to!"

"I wouldn't want you to either. I'd be very uncomfortable, to say the least! Plus, I couldn't see your pretty eyes or kiss your face if you were still in my womb. Your birth was a very good thing. Our family was made more complete by you being born."

"Best family EVER!"

"Yep, but the womb is where God prepared you so you could live in our family. What if someone asked if you wanted to go back into my womb? Would you want to go back?"

"No!"

"Could you go back if you wanted to?"

"There's no way I could fit in your belly again, or even get back in there, but I don't want to anyway!"

"That's good because I prefer you out here too. However, I assure you that when you were in my womb, you were happy there, whether or not you remember being there.

Think about this: What if while you were there, God told you about life on earth? Think you could have imagined it?"

"Hmm, probably not."

"Nope, and that's because all you knew at that time was your life in the womb. Just as now, you only know about life on earth.

You were living in my womb while you were being made ready to live on earth; and when you were ready to live life on this earth, you left my womb and you were born. It's God's design.

And so it is that while here on earth, we can't imagine what heaven is like because this world is all we know. But, just as we're not meant to stay in the womb, we're not meant to stay here on earth either.

When we go to live in heaven, it's similar to our being born into this world. While in the womb we're made ready to live our life on earth; while living on the earth we're being made ready to live forever, either in heaven or, sadly, in hell.

You see, heaven is the home for those who enter through the finished work of Christ and are born again of the Spirit. It's God's provision; he provides the way home. Heaven is the eternal home for the child of God. But if you reject God's gift of life through Christ, then you can't enter into God's eternal home and family because you're not his child. Make sense?"

"Uh huh."

"You're born into heaven through God just as you're born into this world through your mom and dad. How we respond to God's truth on this earth shapes our lives here and prepares us for our eternal home, heaven or hell.

You know, Honey, it's by God's grace that we don't live forever in this sin-filled world. God wants us to live forever where there is no more sin or death. Death is the direct consequence of the first sin, and sin and death are done away with in the last day, right before establishing the new heaven and the new earth, which is absent from any more sin and death!

You know how you said you wouldn't go back to my womb, even if you could?"

"Yeah."

"Well, once we're in heaven, we'll fully understand about life on earth and its preparation stage for our eternal home, and I guarantee you that we'll not want to come back to this earth either. Perhaps, like the womb, we'll know we were once here, but we'll not remember it, and when we see one another, we'll recognize each other but not remember our time together on earth. That's something to ponder."

"What? I don't understand."

"Well, think about this: I shared the womb with my twin brother, yet I don't remember him being in the womb with me, but I know he was there with me. In heaven, we may not remember being here with everyone, but when we see each other, we'll know one another, and even though we can't remember it. we'll know we were togeher while here on earth.

I think we'll also know family and friends who lived before us and those who'll live after us too, because the Bible says that in that day we'll know as we are fully known.

I don't worry with how the details work out; I only know that they do and will. It works out here, and it will there, because God ordained life both here and there."

Matthew 25:31-46; Romans 6:23; John 3:16-21; Matthew; Mark; Luke; John; Romans; Genesis 3:22-24; 1 Corinthians 15:26; Isaiah 25:8; 2 Timothy 1:10; 1 Corinthians 15;1 Peter 3:13; Revelation 21; 1 Cor. 13:12

Preparation Stages
Discussion Questions

1. Just as we're not made to stay in the womb, we're also not made to stay where?

2. How are we born into our new home, heaven?

3. Death is the consequence of what?

4. Are sin and death in the new heaven and new earth?

5. When are sin and death completely removed from our presence?

DYING IS PART OF THIS WORLD

CHAPTER FOUR
Time Here and There

"We've talked about how we get here through a mama and a daddy. Before anyone gets here, they must spend time growing in their mama's womb. They grow there every day, and when they're ready for this world, they're born into it. You see, babies are not meant to stay in their mamas' wombs; they're meant to live here in this world.

You know, when thinking about dying, another

thing to consider is time."

"What do you mean?"

"Well, we live with the constraints of time in this world and how we perceive time here, but God is outside of time. Consider this: We know there's no time in heaven. Forever means forever, not ending, so there's no time to stop. Right?"

"That makes sense."

"We also know from studies surrounding the two atomic clocks that gravity affects time. And continued studies confirm this. Gravity and time are part of this world, and God is outside of both. Since there's no time in heaven, maybe the timing of our death doesn't matter. Perhaps we'll all enter heaven at the same time rather than separately over periods of years. And all because there are no

http://einstein.stanford.edu/content/faqs/gpa_vessot.html

http://www.nist.gov/public_affairs/releases/aluminum-atomic-clock_092310.cfm

http://hyperphysics.phy-astr.gsu.edu/hbase/relativ/airtim.html

http://www.khouse.org/articles/1999/245/

constraints of time in heaven!"

"Huh?"

"I know it's strange to think about, but we know there'll be no time or tears there, and that's hard for us to imagine because that's the world we know."

"Kind of like the baby in the womb thinking about this world?"

"Yes! Or, think about this: What if I do get there first? Perhaps I'll know that you're going to be there eventually, and because there's no time there, the waiting would mean nothing at all to me. Regardless of how it works out, because there are no tears there, we know we won't be sad."

"That makes sense. I'm beginning to understand how we'll not be sad there. That makes me feel better."

"Good. We're almost home. What do you say we put our pj's on and get a piece of cake? Sound good?"

http://www.khouse.org/articles/2013/1123

"Mmmmm! Yeah, Baby!"

"Then it's a plan."

Matthew 25:34; Hebrews 11:16; 2 Corinthians 2; 1 Corinthians 2:7-9; Revelation 21:4

Time Here and There
Discussion Questions

1. Who and what are outside of time?

2. The two atomic clock studies prove what?

3. Gravity and time are part of what?

4. Is there time in heaven?

5. Will there be tears in heaven?

CHAPTER FIVE
Help When Losing Someone

"One more question, Mama."

"Yes?"

"What about being sad here?"

"What?"

"If you go to heaven and I'm here, I'd still be sad

because I'm here without you."

"Well, the one who's still here will be sad. But this world is not our forever home, and when you compare it to our forever home, you see it's just for a short time that we'll miss the ones who've gone before us.

Think about when someone you love takes a trip without you. You're sad when they leave."

"Kind of like the Burdock family?"

"Yes, but you knew you would see them again at the end of the summer. And there was comfort in that. Right?"

"Yes, but without you here, it wouldn't feel short at all."

"I'm sure it wouldn't, but don't forget that Jesus is at the Father's right hand, and he lives forever praying for us. He's also living in us, and the Holy Spirit comforts us, and we also have God's Word that helps us.

Remember, Honey, Jesus came to earth to

set us free from the bondage of fear and death.

The fear of death wants to keep you its prisoner, and that's called bondage. It wants to control you by making you fear it, but when you understand that Jesus demolished death by dying on the cross and rising from the dead, then there's nothing to fear. When Jesus died, death could not hold him. Jesus conquered death and the grave. Dying is part of this world, and it entered through sin, but Jesus has the final word. Death couldn't hold him, and it can't hold us because we belong to him.

Before Adam and Eve sinned, there was no death. Once it came, it was a terrifying thing for Adam and Eve to witness. It's been that way from Adam and Eve to the present time. Everybody knows there's something terribly wrong with death. It hasn't felt natural or right from the very beginning. Deep down we all realize that we were made for eternity. The only hope has always been the promised Savior, Jesus Christ, who would take away the consequences of sin. We can praise God that death will be the last enemy completely destroyed, and in that day it will be forever removed from our presence."

"Wow, I can't wait for that day."

"I know, me too. Here's something else: You know when we see a hearse go by in a funeral procession?"

"Yes."

"You know what I do?"

"What?"

"I pray for those people and all surrounding the loss of that person. I ask God to comfort them and to save any who don't know him. Who knows if anyone else is praying for them?"

"The next time we see that, can I pray for them with you?"

"Yes! God's word tells us to pray without ceasing, and that's a picture of what that looks like.

You see, Honey, while death remains in our presence, we understand that it's an end to the living here but it's also an entrance to our forever home. While it does separate us from our loved ones, that separation is only for a short while. For Christians it's only sad this side of heaven. It's the second death we should really grieve over."

"The second death?!? What? We'll die again? There's more than one death to go through?"

Romans 8:34; John 14:16-18, 26; 2 Thessalonians 2:16-17; Hebrews 2:14-15; 1 Corinthians 15:50-57; Romans 8; 2 Corinthians 1:1-4; Hebrews 2:14-15; 1 Corinthians 15: 50-57; Romans; Genesis 2:17; 3:19; Romans 5:12; 1 Corinthians 15:26; Hebrews 2:14-15; Isaiah 25:8; Hebrews 7:25; Romans 8:34; 2 Timothy 1:10; Revelation 7:17; 21:4-7; 1 Corinthians 15; Genesis 1, 2; 3:15, 21; Romans; Hebrews; John; and the rest of the Scriptures! Revelation 21:4-7; 1 Thessalonians 5:17; Luke 18:1;21:36; Romans 12:12; Ephesian 6:18; Colossians 4:2; 1 Peter 4:7; Philippians 4:6; James 5:16

Help When Losing Someone Discussion Questions

1. Where is Jesus now, and what is he doing?

2. Who and what helps us?

3. Death couldn't hold Jesus, and it can't hold who?

4. While death is in our presence, it's an end to living here in this world but an entrance to where?

5. What should we really grieve over?

CHAPTER 6
The Second Death?

"Notice I said we should grieve over the second death and not fear it. Let me explain. The first death is when we leave this world that's full of sin and death: everybody will experience that one way or another. The second death is for those who come to the end of this life without Christ as their Savior. Without him they cannot be saved from the full measure of death, which is the second death and their final judgment. God tells us that it's appointed to a man once to die, and then the judgment. At that judgment every wicked thing and death itself will be cast into the lake of fire.

God's children will not go through the second death, so no worries, Honey. When God sees you, he sees you in Jesus, and the second death does not apply to those in Jesus. The second death is for those who lived their designated time on earth as if it were their only home, without eternity in mind. That would be like believing our designated time in the womb was our only home."

"Oh I get it. The womb was not where we were meant to stay and this world is not where we are meant to stay. And both prepare us for the life to come."

"Yes. And along with that, God witnesses to everyone through creation that he is God, and he also stamps eternity on all hearts. Everyone has the sense that they were made for eternity. Those who ignore these things will live on earth as if God doesn't exist and will live for this world alone. And because they ignored these witnesses, in the day of judgment they'll stand condemned to the second death, which is eternity in hell. And that's the saddest thing about everything we've discussed.

That's why every day in my prayers I pray for all those who will die that day. I ask God to witness to those who don't know him one last time before they leave this world. And I pray that they'll come to know him. And because he's outside of time... remember that?"

"Yes."

"…I ask him to witness to them no matter how suddenly they die, that they may come to know him. And you know what, Honey?"

"What?"

"When I hear a report of a plane crashing or someone dying, it brings me comfort that I prayed for them.

You see how important it is to live with eternity in mind? We want to know God and his ways. His ways are good, all the time.

Knowing his word and thinking on the things of God gives us peace to make it through the tough times on earth. Jesus said that troubles are part of this world, and death is part of those troubles. However, he also said to rejoice because he overcame this world. This world is NOT our home, so when troubles come, if we face them through Christ, he'll help us."

Hebrews 9:27; Revelation 20:11-15; John 3:16-21; John 16:33; Romans 1

The Second Death
Discussion Questions

1. Judgment comes when?

2. Will God's children experience the second death?

3. At the judgment what will be cast into the lake of fire?

4. What does creation witness to the world?

5. What will happen to those who ignored the witness God gave?

DYING IS PART OF THIS WORLD

CHAPTER SEVEN
God's Economy

"Honey, God has helped me when loved ones have gone on to be with him. He reminds me of all these things and that I'll join them in heaven one day, and in that day what a great reunion that will be!"

"But, Mama, even though I know I'll see you again, I'll still miss you because I see and talk to you every day!"

"I know, Honey, but think about this: Daddy and I taught you to sift everything through the truth of God's word. That memory of us will live on in you. When difficult times come up, and they will, God will remind you of things we taught you that should line up with his word. In fact, if you find that anything does not line up with his word, then you should forget what we said, because God's word is truth. But when those times come up, you'll remember us and be thankful. You may even find yourself thanking me and Dad, out loud, for what we did or for all our precious memories together. That's fine, and that's natural.

These things are similar to when I'm sick and your dad's away. There I am, sick, but I still have to take care of you kids alone. I may be vomiting, and I'll find myself crying out for Mama. In those times I wish she was here to help me. While I was growing up, that's one way she took care of me. Because of that, it can be a natural response to revert back to that cry. I know that I'm not literally calling out to her and expecting her to be here. It's a way of remembering the comfort she brought me in such times. However, God has reminded me in those times that he is always here, and then I cry out to him, my true help.

As we go to God, he comforts us. Then he reminds us of the comfort he brought and brings us, and he asks us to share that same comfort with others so they can be helped."

"Oh, okay. Kind of like how we took cookies to Scott when his dog died, and we prayed for him and told him how God led us to find our new dogs when we were ready for them?"

"Yes, exactly. We comforted him by telling him how God helped and comforted us.

Another example could be you wanting to talk with Dad or me when you have tough things going on or difficult decisions to make. The knee-jerk reaction would be to verbally ask what we—Dad and I—would do in a similar situation. That's normal to do and to feel because that has been a constant source in our relationship.

Parents have such an impact on their childrens' lives. However, we only taught you what God taught us. Therefore, give praise to God and thank him for what we did that was true and right in your life because he's the reason and effort behind our good things.

This may help. Answer this: Who do we both talk to all the time about things going on here?"

"God."

"And where are Mimi and Pops?"

"In heaven with God."

"That's right, and until I see Mimi and Pops again, you know what I do? I ask God to tell them hello and that I love them. This is different from trying to communicate directly with them. I'm not trying to communicate with the dead. God forbids that. I'm asking God, who is with them, to say hello for me, and that I love them."

"You do?"

"Yes."

"Do you think he does?"

"I know that God loves me, and since they're now with him, I don't think he would mind telling them hello from me and that I love them. You see, I'm talking to God, the giver of life, and asking him to tell my loved ones hello for me.

I know they don't want to come back here, but I do think it may make them happy to know their loved ones are keeping the faith and coming their way one day. After all, we're the fruit of their righteous works that continue and will follow them there. Even though they're no longer here, the fruit of their labors continue. Just like the other fruit that we're a part of, the fruit that continues growing from all the great men and women in the Bible. Even though they've been gone for thousands of years, their work impacts our lives, and that fruit continues and will follow them there."

"Like Peter and Paul?"

"Yes, all of them. Way back to Abraham, and before that, way back to the beginning.

Their works are still producing fruit from their works in God.

Remember this: God made us to fellowship with him here and there. He loves and instituted family to show the importance he places on his family. He watches over the womb. He watches over life here on earth. And he'll make everything right when we're in that face-to-face fellowship with him in our eternal home."

"I love God."

"I do too."

"So you ask God to tell Mimi and Pops hello?"

"Yes, in my private prayer time I do. If you'd like, we can start asking him together. I think they smile when he tells them. I'm so looking forward to seeing them, but that'll be right after I greet my Lord!"

"Me too, Mama."

"Remember this for life, Sweetie. When

someone you love leaves this world, if they're Christians, you're not losing them at all. Remember everything I've said, and seek God, and he'll help you with everything. And when you meet new friends who aren't Christians, love them by sharing Jesus with them while there's still time, because God loves them and Jesus died so they can live with him forever.

Does this help you?"

"Yes, Mama, it does. I never thought of these things before."

"Well, God helped me understand first, and that's the only reason I could help you. He's there to help us; we just need to go to him."

"Mama?"

"Yes, Sweetie?"

"What do you think heaven will be like?"

"Oh, Honey, that's a great question, but we're now home. Let's go in and get into our pj's and get that cake. We'll talk more then."

"Ok, you want to race?"

"You're on!"

2 Corinthians 1:3-4; Deuteronomy 18:10-12; Hebrews 12:1-2; Hebrews 11; Genesis 15:5-6; Romans 4:18; Genesis 1:28; 9:1,7; 35:11; Ruth; John; Jeremiah 29:13

God's Economy
Discussion Questions

1. Who do we talk to every day about things going on here?

2. God forbids his children to do what?

3. When a Christian leaves this world, does the fruit of their righteous works stop or continue growing?

4. God made us to fellowship with him where?

5. God loves and instituted what?

OTHER BOOKS IN THE
DISCUSSION BOOK SERIES

Available at www.KaylaJarmon.com